The PURSUIT of GOD
30 DAY DEVOTIONAL

OSIEN SIBANDA

The Pursuit of God, 30 Day Devotinoal

Copyright © 2012 Osien Sibanda

The author has asserted his right to be identified as the author of this work in accordance with the Copyright, Designs and Patents Act 1988. All rights reserved. No part of this publication may be reproduced, stored in a retrieval system, or transmitted, in any form or by any means, electronic, mechanical, photocopying, recording or otherwise without the prior permission of Sibanda Publishing.

All Scripture quotations, unless otherwise indicated, are taken from the Holy Bible, New International Version, UK edition, copyright © 1973, 1978, 1984 by International Bible Society. Published by Hodder and Stoughton. Used by permission. All rights reserved.

Scripture quotations marked NKJV are taken from the Holy Bible, New King James Version®, copyright © 1982 by Thomas Nelson, Inc. Used by permission.

All rights reserved.

Scripture quotations marked KJV are taken from the Holy Bible, King James Version, Cambridge University Press, Oxford University Press, HarperCollins and the Queen's Printers.

Scripture quotations marked NLT are taken from the Holy Bible, New Living Translation, copyright 1996. Used by permission of Tyndale House Publishers, Inc., Wheaton, Illinois 60189. All rights reserved.

A catalogue record for this book is available from the British Library.

Published in the United Kingdom by Sibanda Publishing.

ISBN: 978-0-9561175-8-8

Dedication

I would like to dedicate this 30 day devotional to Pastor Agu Irukwu. Had it not been for your heart and desire to pursue God, and your encouragement for me to join the 30 day fast, this devotional would not have been written. As you continue to pursue him, may he satisfy the longings of your heart.

Acknowledgements

Writing this devotional has been a pleasant journey partly because of the invaluable support, feedback and inspiration from different people who have come alongside to help. Special thanks go to my precious wife and friend Fatima Sibanda. Thank you for all your input and editing.

Sarah Masengo, thank you for designing and preparing the devotional for printing. I could not have done this without you. God bless you! Ayanda and Lebo my daughters, thank you for enriching my life the way you do. To Pastor Gerri Di Somma, thank you for the valuable insights from your devotional. To our church family, God's House International Centre, thank you for reading and your encouragement through your follower ship. God bless you!

Contents

Inroduction 9

1 Studying The Word 11

2 Hearing God 13

3 Obeying God 15

4 Serving In God's House 17

5 Living Life Selflessly 19

6 Regecting The Stonghold of Debt 21

7 Becoming Debt Free 23

8 The Help Of God 25

9 Leading Our Community Morally 27

10 Living As a Light to the World 29

11 Obedience in Giving 31

12 Obedience in Giving to Others 33

13 Obedience in Tithing 35

14 Christlikeness 37

15 Knowing Christ 39

16	Being Honest In All Things	41
17	Conducting Your Life Well	43
18	Managing Your Thoughts	45
19	A Right Heart Attitude	47
20	Being Doers of the Word	49
21	Applying God's Wisdom	51
22	Developing the Fruit of the Spirit	53
23	The Fruit of Goodness	55
24	The Fruit of Gentleness	57
25	The Fruit of Faithfulness	59
26	The Fruit of Patience	61
27	Practising Kindness	63
28	Practincing Self-Control	65
29	Walking in Peace	67
30	Walking in Love	69

Introduction

The Prophet Isaiah encourages us to *"Seek the Lord while He may be found, and to call upon Him while He is near."* (**Isaiah 55:6**). This implies that there are times when the Lord can be far; and there are also times when the Lord may not be found. The apostle James also instructs us to *"draw near to God and he will draw near to us"* (**James 4:8**). The pursuit of God is about drawing near to him continually. Staying close to him and following him closely enables us to get his heart for us and for others. It also helps us to stay in close proximity without losing him.

Seeking God must be intentional. As a result, setting a period of time to seek him must be a discipline God's people must take seriously. The Psalmist says, *"my heart longs for you like a deer longs for water"* (**Psalm 42:1**). A deer longing for water will not stop its search until it finds that water to quench its thirst. Pursuing God is longing for him and taking the necessary steps and discipline to know him more until we know him. The apostle Paul wrote, *"That I may know him..."* (**Philippians 3:10-14**). There should be a longing to know God more in every believer! This devotional has been written to inspire and encourage to you in your pursuit for God. I pray that as we seek him daily, we will find him daily and walk with him daily!

1

STUDYING THE WORD

Studying in any field results in more knowledge and 'knowledge is power'. The Word of God must be studied and known by every believer. In **Hosea 4:6** God says, *"... my people are destroyed from lack of knowledge. Because you have rejected knowledge, I also reject you as my priests..."* God desires that His children know Him and avoid being deceived. Most of Jesus' teachings show how He had the knowledge of the Father and how He knew the Word. During Jesus's temptation in the desert, Satan could not deceive Him because He knew the Word (**Luke 4:1-13**).

Speaking about the devil, Daniel said, *"With flattery he will corrupt those who have violated the covenant, but the people who know their God will firmly resist him"* (**Daniel 11:32**). The study of the Word gives us knowledge that enables us to avoid falling for the tricks of the enemy.

Jesus experienced the devil's flattery in **Luke 4:9-11**: *"'If you are the Son of God,' he said, 'throw yourself down from here. For it is written: 'He will command his angels concerning you to guard you carefully... so that you will not strike your foot against a stone.'"* This was blatant flattery by Satan. Jesus knew this and refused to fall for it, and He succeeded in His mission, hence His words on the cross: *"It is finished"* (**John 19:30**). The people who know their God will be strong and resist the devil. Jesus confirms that He knew God in **John 4:22**: *"You Samaritans worship what you do not know; we worship what we do know..."* Studying the Word helps us to know whom we worship.

The apostle Paul tells the young Timothy, *"Do your best to present yourself to God as one approved... who correctly handles the word of truth"* (**2 Timothy 2:15**). To approve is to acknowledge as acceptable. Jesus was acceptable to God, who said, *"This is my Son, whom I love; with him I am well pleased"* (**Matthew 3:17**). Studying, increasing our knowledge and applying that knowledge to our daily living will cause God to approve us as His acceptable representatives on earth. God will give us more responsibility, more influence and more power, depending on our level of maturity through applying the Word.

The book of Proverbs encourages us: *"The beginning of wisdom is this: get wisdom. Though it cost all you have, get understanding"* (**Proverbs 4:7**). We also understand that wisdom is given by God, according to **James 1:5**: *"If any of you* *lacks wisdom, you should ask God, who gives generously to all without finding fault, and it will be given to you."*

All these important truths are in the Word. Studying the Word is crucial for our success as children of God. Even the very faith that we are living by comes from hearing the Word, according to **Romans 10:17**.

> **REFLECTION TIME**
>
> Repent for your relaxed approach to the Word. It is key to your success. It is key to growing your faith and it is key to resisting the devil and to pleasing God. Ask God to help you to be disciplined and consistent in your study of the Word.

2

HEARING GOD

As God's people, it is important for us to hear what the Father has for us at various stages of our Christian walk. That is what will help us lead a successful life in our journey of faith.

The first way in which God has spoken to us is through His Word, in both the Old and New Testaments. **Hebrews 1:1-2** says: *"In the past God spoke to our ancestors through the prophets at many times and in various ways, but in these last days he has spoken to us by his Son..."*

What has God spoken to us by His Son? Many things, as seen in the New Testament. But one of the things Jesus said was that we ought always to pray and not lose heart (**Luke 18:1**). He also taught that we must forgive others when we stand to pray before the Father (**Mark 11:25**), if we want the Father to forgive us.

Another important teaching is that we must be led by the Spirit, and for us to be led by the Spirit we need to be able to hear Him. The Bible tells us in **Acts 8:29** that the Spirit said to Philip, *"Go to that chariot and stay near it."* Philip had to know when the Spirit of God was sending him on assignment. His ability to hear God made him successful in his mission and the eunuch was saved and baptised.

God is still talking to this day, but sometimes we do not hear because of the many voices that compete for our attention. We need to block our ears to the other voices by finding quiet times with God, where we can pray for the grace to hear God for ourselves. Then we will be more successful in our mission.

1 Kings 19:11-18 makes us realise that God speaks in a small still voice, and to hear that we must be tuned to Him with all concentration.

REFLECTION TIME

Find a quiet place away from distractions of your daily routine and talk to God in prayer, meditation and in silence. As you pray, ask Him to speak to you and show you what you should be doing in the kingdom for the remaining six months of this year. Pray that you may hear Him this year.

3

Obeying God

In **Matthew 21:28-32**, Jesus gave a parable about obedience involving two sons who were given an instruction and responded differently. He then wanted His listeners to decide which son did the will of God. In other words, *"Which of these sons was obedient?"*

When God speaks to His people, be it through sermons, counsel, a still small voice or even nature, He expects them to obey. Obedience to God is the first step to success in our walk with Him. It confirms our faith and trust in God. **Isaiah 1:19** says, *"If you are willing and obedient [to God], you will eat the good things of the land."* We must not only obey what is comfortable and pleasurable to us but must learn to obey all of God's instructions.

James teaches us not to be hearers of the Word only. He encourages us rather to be doers of the Word as well (**James 1:22**). Having heard from God, there is a follow-on that requires action and that action shows that we love God. As Jesus said, *"If you love me, keep my commands"* (**John 14:15**). This is one of the greatest tests in any believer's life. To obey God!

We want to ask God to help us to trust and obey Him in these last six months of the year. It's easy to claim that we love God, but to truly love Him is to follow His instructions daily, not just when we are happy or when we feel like it.

The two sons I mentioned in the first paragraph were told to go and work in the field. The first son refused outright, but later changed his mind and went. The other son said that he would go, but did not go. Which of these two boys did the Father's will?

May the Lord help us not to live by good intentions: "I intended to come to church, I intend to pray, I intend to give to the poor, I intend to and intend to..." Good intentions are not enough. They will never make you successful in your walk with God, because He requires obedience and action. Remember, "The road to hell is paved with good intentions."

REFLECTION TIME

Ask God to reveal areas in your life where you have disobeyed Him and begin your obedience from there. This is the only way you will be successful in your Christian walk. Let us obey God.

4

SERVING IN GOD'S HOUSE

Yesterday we looked at the role of obedience and the blessings it brings to those who are obedient. **Isaiah 1:19** comes to mind to consolidate this. Further down in verse 20, Isaiah warns, *"...but if you resist and rebel, you will be devoured by the sword."* We should not be one of those who refuse to obey the Lord.

Serving in the church is an area where most of the work is left for the "faithful few", yet we all profess to love God, hear Him and supposedly obey Him. Looking at the practical application, however, we can see that not all the hands of the church members are on the "plough." Today we want to review this in our prayer and reflection as we ask God to help us to get involved in His house, beginning this month.

It is important for believers to get involved in their local church, because God has designed the church in such a way that it is sustained by the gifts of the believers, according to **Ephesians 4:16**. Inactive Christians' failure or refusal to serve not only deprives the church of the growth that can only be attained through their gifts and involvement, it also affects their own success and growth. This ultimately results in unhealthy, limping, weak, ineffective and docile believers who are not flourishing.

Psalm 92:13 states that those who are *"planted in the house of the Lord, they will flourish in the courts of our God."* To be planted in the house is not for show or for only attending on a Sunday. Rather, it is about involvement! Jesus used the analogy of hands on the plough to explain the importance of serving in the house of God *"No one who puts a hand to the plough and looks back is fit for service in the kingdom of God"* (**Luke 9:62**). In other words, we must get involved and continue to focus on what the plough is tilling. This is the essence of **Psalm 92:13** and serving in the church.

King David understood the importance of serving in the house of God and the success and blessings this brings, so much so that he wrote: *"Better is one day in your courts than a thousand elsewhere; I would rather be a doorkeeper in the house of my God than dwell in the tents of the wicked"* (**Psalm 84:10**). David preferred to guard the door of the house of God, if all other positions were filled. He did not stay at home. How is your service to your local church?

This is what you should look at today as you pray for God's help, so that you can put your priorities right in the area of obedience as far as your attitude to service is concerned. Service in the house of God is an aspect of obedience to God. You cannot obey Him and yet fail to serve. The parable of the two sons in **Matthew 21:28-30** is also about service.

Begin to serve in the local church that you attend .The rewards are plentiful. The Bible says that when you are planted you will flourish. To flourish is to prosper and to develop. You will be successful, productive and fruitful, as **Psalm 1** points out, *"That person is like a tree planted by streams of water, which yields its fruit in season and whose leaf does not wither – whatever they do prospers."* Serving in your local church will make you prosperous!

I would like to encourage you to look into your life and consider your service from today to the end of the year.

REFLECTION TIME

Find out what your gifts and skills are, then see where you can deploy them in your local church. Pray for God to help you to rise up and serve. Look out for the departmental leaders and speak to them, then join the one that suits your gifts best. Get involved and remain faithful, and then see if you will not flourish!

5

LIVING LIFE SELFLESSLY

Jesus gave us an important principle to live by in **Mark 8:34** (NKJV): *"Whoever desires to come after Me [or be my follower], let him deny himself, and take up his cross, and follow Me."* The cross was an instrument of total self-denial for Christ, where His choice and power were totally and willingly given up for others.

Jesus was crucified for the sin He did not commit. He went to the cross in order to save us because we could not save ourselves. He was prepared to take our place. The Bible wants us to approach our Christian walk in a similar way. The apostle Paul puts it this way: *"Don't look out only for your own interests, but take an interest in others, too"* (**Philippians 2:4, NLT**).

By now we should be aware that we don't go to heaven with any of our earthly possessions. All our achievements, money, skills, talents, qualifications and gifts are to be used to bless others, in order to demonstrate the kingdom. It's people that we will take to heaven, hence the call for us to consider and minister to them. The impact we have on them will be a testimony of how we led selfless lives on earth. The world is different, in that people are generally focused on themselves, but in the kingdom it's different. Focussing on others is an expression of love and it takes commitment and self-denial.

Jesus demonstrated that such a life is possible when He walked the streets of Jerusalem and wherever He went. Nothing He did benefitted Him directly. It was for the benefit of the lepers, the blind, the lame, the poor, the woman with the issue of blood, the Roman centurion, and so on. Jesus put the interests of others first and that caused many to come into the kingdom.

If we approach our service in the kingdom in the same manner, we can also have the same impact. Jesus literally gave His life on the cross to benefit people. We may not have to go to the cross, but our attitude to others and those in need can be our cross for them. Many people testify of Jesus' kindness and love. They can also testify of your love and kindness if you begin to look, treat and relate to them through a selfless heart.

Serving in the house of God requires self-denial. As we work with others, there will be times when we will encounter situations that require us to look to the interests of others first. Let us pray that God will help us to live our lives selflessly. That way, we will not manipulate people. We will not be rude. We learn to be gentle when we are serving with others in mind.

> **REFLECTION TIME**
>
> Ask God to give you the grace to be compassionate and ready to go the extra mile for others. Look out for opportunities to do something good for someone this week. You don't have to limit that to one person or this week only, but consider making this part of your daily life. See what testimonies will come out of that. The Bible says God is glorified when we do such things.

6
REJECTING THE STRONGHOLD OF DEBT

Debt does not need defining at all. I'm sure most of us have had a brush with it, one way or the other. A popular Finnish proverb says: *"No investment is as secure as a repaid debt."* Many people unfortunately get into debt easily and then fail to repay, putting themselves into a further predicament, resulting in a total mess of their lives.

Proverbs 22:7 teaches us that *"the borrower is slave [or servant] to the lender"*. The apostle Paul reminds us in **1 Corinthians 7:23** that we *"were bought at a price; do not become slaves of human beings."* Slaves are not free to do as they please, let alone serve God the way they want. You cannot give to God when you are in debt. You cannot tithe happily when you are in debt.

Getting out of debt must be the objective of every believer if we are to do the work of God joyfully and unrestrained. The deception when getting into debt is, "I will earn enough in the future to pay it off." This is very presumptuous, and the scriptures warn us against this in the book of James: *"Now listen, you who say, 'Today or tomorrow we will go to this or that city, spend a year there, carry on business and make money.' Why, you do not even know what will happen tomorrow..."* (**James 4:13-14**).

The Word of God makes it clear that God's plan for us is to be free from debt. This is important, because the blessings of being debt free go far beyond avoiding slavery to someone else. They extend to the spiritual realm as well. It's easier to obey the prompting to give when you don't have debts to think about. It's easier to consider others when you are not in debt yourself. It's easier to serve in God's house if you are not in debt. It's easier to turn down an extra shift and attend prayer when you are not in debt. "No one who is financially bound is spiritually free" (Larry Burkett).

As we seek the Lord in prayer, let us review our attitude to debt. We must stop embracing debt as our kinsman. We must stop running for loans that take away a lot more from us in interest. In **John 8:36** Jesus teaches, *"So if the Son sets you free, you will be free indeed."* This includes debt. Ask God to give you wisdom in handling money because money can be easily spent but hard to earn. The words of the poet Ogden Nash come to mind: *"O money, money, money, I'm not necessarily one of those who think thee holy, but I often stop to wonder how thou canst go out so fast when thou comest in so slowly."*

> **REFLECTION TIME**
>
> If you are in debt, look at your life to see how this has affected your life negatively, and begin to ask God for a way out. As you pray, identify a strategy to begin to escape from debt. If you are not in financial debt, you may like to look at **Romans 13:8**, which teaches that we owe others love. Find ways of paying that debt as you prepare your heart to be a vessel for God to use.

7

BECOMING DEBT FREE

The children of Israel were assured a debt-free life if they obeyed God. That should be the same with us because we serve the same God, who does not change. This is what He said to the children of Israel in **Deuteronomy 15:4-6**: *"...there need be no poor people among you, for in the land the Lord your God is giving you to possess as your inheritance, he will richly bless you, if only you fully obey the Lord your God and are careful to follow all these commands I am giving you today. For the Lord your God will bless you as he has promised, and you will lend to many nations but will borrow from none. You will rule over many nations but none will rule over you."*

This is God's promise to those who obey Him. If you find yourself in debt, realise that this is not the will of God for you. If you are drowning in debt to the point of not opening certain letters that come through your door, in fear of final demands and a threat by the bailiffs, you need to ask God for help very quickly. You must gain back your financial freedom.

The first step into that freedom is to stop borrowing, period! Stop incurring more debt. This is a difficult step to take, but if you realise that you are out of God's will by being in debt, then that should be motivation enough to get out of debt. Pray and ask God for discipline. Don't spend money that you don't have because it makes you a slave who is not in control of his finances. Buy now and pay later schemes don't work to your advantage. They cause you to spend your future income, enslaving you to the lenders. Refuse to borrow willy nilly.

After stopping borrowing, one next important step is to reduce spending. Spending eats away your money and prevents you from filling up the "debt hole", so find ways to reduce spending. Ever heard the saying, 'Money talks... but all mine ever says is goodbye!'? Don't allow your money to bid you goodbye again until you have cleared all your debts. Never allow your money to leave you for useless purchases. Purchasing on your credit card does not help you realise that you don't have money in your account, especially if you want to get out of debt. You might need to consider paying for your expenses in cash, and when the cash runs out you wait for the end of the month.

Another important step in this journey to financial freedom is prayer. Never underestimate the power of prayer. When we pray, we ask God for help and He certainly does come through for those who trust in Him.

In **2 Kings 4:1-7** there is a story about a woman who was left in so much debt that it threatened the lives of her two sons by her husband. The debts were so great that she could not imagine herself paying them until she took her case to God through the prophet, Elisha. God intervened and the boys were not only spared but the debt was paid as well. God answers prayer. As we look to clean up our act in the area of debt, may we realise that debt is not a blessing but a curse, according to **Deuteronomy 28:44**, and the earlier you realise that the quicker you will get out. God will help you if you ask for His help.

> ### REFLECTION TIME
> Meditate on the reason you are in debt and begin to eliminate it. Ask the Lord to help you deal with it and don't entangle yourself again. You might have to work extra to clear your bills or cut your spending. Whatever it takes, use this as a way to engage God in order to be free.

8

THE HELP OF GOD

David is one man who knew the importance of having a good relationship with God in his life, and always sought His presence. In **Psalm 121:2**, David states that his help comes from the Lord. He then explains why he can rely on God for that help. It's because God is *"the Maker of heaven and earth"* (the last phrase of verse 2). This is important because everything David ever contended with in life took place on the earth that God created, so he was sure to receive help in times of trouble.

God *"will not let your foot slip"* (verse 3). He does not allow us to lose the ground we have gained if we know our place in Him. This is the reason David was not afraid of his enemies. The Lord who kept him did not slumber (verses 3-4). He watched over David 24 hours a day.

Our relationship with God can develop to the same level if we continue to seek the Lord, for God rewards those who seek Him. Do you want the Lord to help you? Then learn to seek Him. If you do, He will not let your foot slip. He will be your keeper, He will be your shade (verse 5). The Lord will preserve you from evil, if you seek Him and walk with Him. Abraham walked with God and He preserved him from evil, even in foreign lands. Desire to seek the Lord this last part of the year, and see Him help you to regain the ground you may have lost earlier this year.

The Lord preserves your soul. The Lord preserves your going out and your coming in, if you learn to delight in Him. He still looks for companions and friends till this day, but they must seek Him. Those who find Him will not be moved! **Psalm 125** says those who trust in the Lord shall be like Mount Zion, *"which cannot be shaken..."* (verse 1). You can become solid and stable, through putting your trust in the Lord.

Jesus also taught us to seek first the kingdom of God and His righteousness, and then the things we need will be added to us (**Matthew 6:33**). Where do you look in times of trouble and stress? David looked to God and received assurance that the Lord would defend him. How confident are you about the help of God in your life? God is the helper of those who trust and seek Him. There are challenges in life that require God's intervention, but you should not wait for problems before you call on Him. Walking daily with Him puts you in a position where God defends you, because you give Him pleasure.

> **REFLECTION TIME**
>
> Pray for a closer walk with God. Ask Him to help you develop a special relationship with Him, whereby you will be confident of His help at any time. Learn to lift up your eyes to Him in confidence because of your relationship with Him, as an obedient child who depends on his Father.

9

LEADING OUR COMMUNITY MORALLY

Jesus said we are the light and the salt of the world, according to **Matthew 5:13-14**. Our world implies our sphere of influence. This means we must reflect the heart, spirit and life of Jesus Christ wherever we are. One of the major issues Jesus stood for was morality and justice.

Isaiah 61:8 reads: *"For I, the Lord, love justice..."* In **Psalm 37:30** we learn that the *"mouths of the righteous utter wisdom, and their tongues speak what is just."* We do this in our communities as we demonstrate the life of God. God loves justice. We as His children must love justice because we are the voice of God in our communities. We are His hands and feet. We must be God's mouthpiece in matters of morality and justice. Unfortunately, this has not been so for many believers. Instead of leading in morality, we have been the cause of some of the immorality and injustice in our communities and places of work.

As we seek the Lord in prayer, let us ask for God's help in this area so that we can lead our communities towards godliness. We must begin to address and challenge some of the injustice where we live. Sometimes this takes more than prayer, it takes action and involvement. Consider getting to know your local councillors and members of parliament, so that you can begin to engage with them as well as pray for them. If all of us are actively involved, there can be positive change in the way things are done.

Remember that Daniel and the three Hebrew boys changed the legislation from within the Babylonian leadership structure. They stood for justice and accomplished it. Esther did the same, and so did Joseph. We want to deliberately begin to know what is happening in our communities, with the hope of shining the light of Christ into them as we get involved practically. The mouth of the righteous speaks wisdom, according to **Psalm 37**, and in **2 Corinthians 5:21** we learn that we have become the righteousness of God in Christ. Because of this, our tongue must speak justice in our communities. Our mouths must speak wisdom.

REFLECTION TIME

What have you been speaking into your community? Has your tongue been rising against injustice or have you been quiet? You are meant to represent your Father in combating injustice. Find out the state of your community, schools, shops, clinics, police stations and any other governmental structures. Begin to pray for them, that God's justice and righteousness may prevail. See how you can get involved in a practical way in order to shine the light of Christ. You are the salt and light in that community. Pray that you may influence your community in a tangible way.

10
Living As A Light To The Community

In **Acts 13:47** the Lord says: *"I have made you a light for the Gentiles, that you may bring salvation to the ends of the earth."* The Message version of the Bible translates this as: *"I've set you up as light to all nations. You'll proclaim salvation to the four winds and seven seas!"*

As Christians, our lives should continually demonstrate a high standard of morality and godliness, because God has set us up as a light to our communities. This is the light that we are meant to shine in front of those who live in darkness in our street, town or nation. Our lifestyle should be evidently marked by qualities of decency, honesty, goodness, love, kindness, mercy, gentleness, compassion and trustworthiness. This is our light and it must be seen in our community. A lifestyle like this will always stand out in an immoral and ungodly environment.

We attain this lifestyle by living according to the principles God has given us in His Word. The apostle Paul reminds Timothy about the importance of these principles if he is to shine this light in his community: *"And the Lord's servant must not be quarrelsome but must be kind to everyone, able to teach, not resentful. Opponents must be gently instructed, in the hope that God will grant them repentance leading them to a knowledge of the truth, and that they will come to their senses and escape from the trap of the devil, who has taken them captive to do his will"* (**2 Timothy 2:24-26**). Certain parts of your community have been taken captive by the devil, who leads people to do all the immoral things they are doing. Your life can be the light that shows them their mistakes, but if you don't light that light before them, they will perish.

How do you view your community and the unrighteousness in it? Do you see the evil as the devil's doing or as just their way of life? Do you realise that they are in bondage and they need your prayers and your voice to help them out? God has planted you there to be His witness and ambassador. Don't be caught up in the things of the world and forget your assignment. You have been planted as God's light! Many times we don't realise our mission and end up behaving like the world. Determine to be different.

The Word tells us that God has deliberately set us up as a light in those communities in order to declare His salvation. Do you realise that? You must be a light to the children, a light to the aged, a light to the confused youth and a light to the community and its leaders, who may have no idea how to bring morality back to their communities. If you ask God for a strategy, He will give you the grace to begin to engage with individuals and you will begin to be fruitful and effective in your community.

You don't have to wait for an evangelism project or event to begin to do that. Your light is already shining. You must just remember that you have been sent as a moral agent and begin from the little things, with your neighbours or your local shop owner, etc.

REFLECTION TIME

Meditate upon **Acts 13:47** and see where you have been lacking in shining your light. Ask God to strengthen your light and give you boldness to engage your community. Ask for opportunities to correct certain immoral things in gentleness and love. You will be amazed at how ready some people are for godliness. Remember the words of Jesus in **Matthew 9:37**: *"The harvest is plentiful but the workers are few."* Determine to be one of those "few" in your community who will labour for righteousness, and the Lord will grant that desire.

11

Obedience In Giving

"Jesus sat down opposite the place where the offerings were put and watched the crowd putting their money into the temple treasury" **Mark 12:41**. The passage continues to describe how He watched the people as they gave, and then shared His conclusion with His disciples: *"Truly I tell you, this poor widow has put more into the treasury than all the others"* (verse 43). Jesus compared the giving of people into the treasury, so there is no reason why He cannot do the same in our day.

Pastor Johnny Hunt from First Baptist Church Woodstock Atlanta often says you are most like Jesus when you give generously. Jesus is a great example of a giver. From giving up His heavenly life, He went on to feed multitudes, heal those who were sick, give freedom to those who were oppressed, and ultimately give His own life on the cross. **Philippians 2:9** concludes: *"Therefore God exalted him to the highest place and gave him the name that is above every name..."* God honoured Him after He gave up everything for us. Jesus's giving is still benefiting the nations thousands of years later.

Giving is an act that very few people practise naturally, but it is at the heart of God's plan for our blessing and prosperity. That is why we are taught to give. It's like going to school. For some it's a burden they would not willingly want to bear, but they must still go to school and be taught what they will need for the future. Never underestimate the power of obedience to giving.

Proverbs 11:24-25 teaches, *"One person gives freely, yet gains even more; another withholds unduly, but comes to poverty. A generous person will prosper..."* As you continue to look into your life and the response you give to God in the area of giving, ask yourself, *"How am I doing as far as giving to the treasury is concerned?"* The apostle Paul reminded his leaders about the importance of giving in **Acts 20:35**: *"In everything I did, I showed you that by this kind of hard work we must help the weak, remembering the words the Lord Jesus himself said: 'It is more blessed to give than to receive.'"* Do you believe this? Then take it seriously from now on!

REFLECTION TIME

Look into your heart. Review your attitude to giving, if you were not taking this seriously in the past. Pray that God helps you not to hoard things that you can lose anytime. Begin to develop a lifestyle of giving, and be an investor in the treasury of God.

12

GIVING TO OTHERS

Jesus said: *"Give to the one who asks you, and do not turn away from the one who wants to borrow from you"* (**Matthew 5:42**). We may not realise that this is a command from scripture but it is, and it must be obeyed fully by everyone who claims to be a believer.

One of the blessings of obedience is that we will lend to others but not have to borrow (**Deuteronomy 15:6**). Finding yourself in a position where people borrow from you is a blessing, and Jesus says we should not turn anybody away.

Giving to others is part of obedience to the teachings of the Christian faith and so must be put into practice. You cannot do these things if you are in debt. You might be thinking that this faith thing is taking away all your money. No! Remember what Jesus said to the rich young ruler who wanted to follow Him? (**Matthew 19:16-22**). Our dependence must be on God, not what is in our hand, if we understand faith. Jesus wanted the young ruler to know this, so He told him to give his money away: *"If you want to be perfect, go, sell your possessions and give to the poor, and you will have treasure in heaven. Then come, follow me."*

God measures things in a different manner from us. The great Bible teacher Andrew Murray lamented our approach to giving in these words: "How different our standard is from Christ's. We ask how much a man gives. Christ asks how much he keeps." That is why Jesus commended the widow who gave just two small coins in **Mark 12:41-44**. Jesus said everyone else who gave had a lot remaining for them to live on, but the woman, *"out of her poverty, put in everything – all she had to live on"* (erse 44). Giving to others is a way of building up our treasure in heaven. If we believed this, we would be happy to give away virtually everything in this life, all the time.

The other important thing about giving to others is explained in **Matthew 25:35-40**: *"'For I was hungry and you gave me something to eat, I was thirsty and you gave me something to drink, I was a stranger and you invited me in, I needed clothes and you clothed me, I was ill and you looked after me, I was in prison and you came to visit me.' Then the righteous will answer him, 'Lord, when did we see you hungry and feed you, or thirsty and give you something to drink? When did we see you a stranger and invite you in, or needing clothes* *and clothe you? When did we see you ill or in prison and go to visit you?' The King will reply, 'Truly I tell you, whatever you did for one of the least of these brothers and sisters of mine, you did for me.'"*

The challenge is that, among the people with needs that we meet, we don't know which one is God in disguise. Are you aware that some of these needy people are actually sent by God because He has given you everything that you have? He expects you to extend that grace to others. If you waste your resources on selfish things and debt, you are not being a good steward and you not building up treasure in heaven. As a believer, what you own belongs to God, and He can call on you to use it for others so that He can be glorified.

In **Matthew 5:16** Jesus says, *"Let your light shine before others, that they may see your good deeds and glorify your Father in heaven."* These good works are the hospital visits, the food, the clothing and whatever other people will ask of you, as mentioned in **Matthew 25**.

> ### REFLECTION TIME
> As you seek God for a closer walk with Him this month, pray that you will not miss an opportunity to minister to someone who will matter on Judgement Day. Determine not to look at your resources by what you have given already. Pray to be sensitive to the Spirit and the needs of others as far as giving is concerned. This will form part of our reward on Judgement Day.

13

Obedience In Tithing

Tithing is one of those practices that usually reveal a clear divide in understanding and view in many Christians. Tithing is about giving the first ten per cent of your income to God for the use of the church, by those whose hearts are devoted to God for the furtherance of His kingdom.

In **Matthew 6:21** Jesus says, *"For where your treasure is, there your heart will be also."* We have already seen that Jesus told the rich young ruler to give to the poor so that he would have treasure in heaven. If our treasure was truly in heaven as we profess, tithing would be a pleasure.

J. D. Rockefeller, an American business magnate, once said, "I never would have been able to tithe the first million dollars I ever made if I had not tithed my first salary, which was about $1.50 per week." There goes a businessman who understood God's principles, and he prospered. Many intend to tithe when they get a big chunk of money. It will never happen. We must learn to honour God from the small things so that when big things come our way, we are already humble and well trained to obey Him.

Tithing is a way of honouring God so that His kingdom can be sustained and godly influence prevail. Jesus never stopped New Testament believers from tithing, as many people want to claim. Otherwise, how did He expect the church to operate? In **Matthew 23:23** Jesus says, *"Woe to you, teachers of the law and Pharisees, you hypocrites! You give a tenth of your spices – mint, dill and cumin. But you have neglected the more important matters of the law – justice, mercy and faithfulness. You should have practised the latter, without neglecting the former."* Tithing must not be neglected, according to Jesus. We must be obedient in this area!

But tithing must not be a 'box-ticking' exercise to make us feel more spiritual than the next person. It must be done with the right motive, of gratitude to God for all He gives to us. In **Luke 18:9-14**, Jesus tells a parable about a man who fasted twice a week and gave his tithe, but was not justified before God because of his wrong, self-righteous attitude. God wants us to obey His counsel in full, with humility and grace. We don't do it for the praises of men but to honour God.

If you are heavily in debt, you will be grieved by having to give away ten per cent of your income. Your income has already been stolen, hence the pain. The tithe should be set aside before any of your income is spent, and then you are left with the 90 per cent for yourself and other requirements. People of the Old Testament believed and understood this principle. Rockefeller also understood it and he prospered.

The apostle Paul taught the people, *"On the first day of every week, each one of you should set aside a sum of money in keeping with your income, saving it up, so that when I come no collections will have to be made"* (**1 Corinthians 16:2**). This was for church use and every believer was expected to be involved. James MacDonald wrote, "First things belong to God. The first day of the week belongs to God. The first hour of the day belongs to God. The first portion of your income belongs to God. When you make God first, He can help you."

Tithing is not just a financial issue. It's a matter of obedience, faith and trust in God. It is a spiritual principle. If the Word commands us to tithe and we choose not to, we are disobeying God. How do we expect God to bless us financially, if we are not obedient to Him?

> ### REFLECTION TIME
> Pray and ask for an understanding of trusting God and be determined to trust God with your tithe. Move away from selective obedience to full obedience. Galatians tells us that God is not mocked. Trust Him and learn to totally surrender in your finances, whether that means starting tithing or being generous to others and the church.

14

CHRISTLIKENESS

The life of a Christian derives its nature and character from the person of Christ. We must be like Christ in virtually everything we are and everything we do, if we are to be respected as believers. The believers were first called Christians in Antioch because they walked and lived like Christ (**Acts 11:26**). We must also grow and imitate Christ to such an extent that people in our spheres of influence can see Christ in us.

Paul told the Galatians that he was praying for them so that they would be like Christ: *"My dear children, for whom I am again in the pains of childbirth until Christ is formed in you…"* (**Galatians 4:19**). The idea of Christlikeness is that you become like Christ in your conduct.

Our prayer and focus should be Christlikeness. Being like Christ helps us to live His life and walk in the authority that He delegated to us. This also helps us demonstrate the kindness, love and compassion that was modelled by Jesus. We attain this likeness by studying Jesus' life and emulating it. Paul prayed that Christ would be formed in the Galatians, and He must be formed in us as well. Just like Paul prayed for this, we can also pray that Christ be formed in us.

Paul said that he emulated the life of Christ: *"Follow my example, as I follow the example of Christ"* (**1 Corinthians 11:1**). One of the areas where we can imitate Christ is in His obedience to the Father. The apostle John teaches that *"what we will be has not yet been made known. But we know that when Christ appears, we shall be like him…"* (**1 John 3:2**). It is important for us to aim to be like Christ, because those who will make it to heaven are those who are like Christ (thankfully, when God looks on us He sees Christ, because of Jesus' death for us). Those who overcome temptation are those who are like Christ. Those who overcome sin are those who are like Christ. Those who overcome the devil are those who are like Christ.

Attaining Christlikeness must be our goal as believers. It is good for us, it is good for our faith walk, and it is good for our missionary work. The devil will know and respect you if you are like Christ. The work of the ministry requires us to be like Christ.

The sons of Sceva tried to do the work of the ministry without Christlikeness and the devil gave them a torrid time. *"One day the evil spirit answered them, 'Jesus I know, and Paul I know about, but who are you?'"* (**Acts 19:15**). The matter did not end there! In verse 16 we are told, *"Then the man who had the evil spirit jumped on them and overpowered them all. He gave them such a beating that they ran out of the house naked and bleeding."* Without the nature of Christ in us, we will be overpowered and destroyed by sin and every evil work. The evil spirit knew Jesus, as well as the Paul who imitated Him. This is the same Paul who tells us that his prayer and priority is that Christ must be formed in every believer. You must be like Christ for you to overcome evil and help others to overcome. **Romans 12:21** teaches us, *"Do not be overcome by evil, but overcome evil with good."* This will not happen until we attain Christlikeness in our lives.

REFLECTION TIME

Determine to obey God in everything you do until your family, community and fellow Christians testify about your faith. Pray that God will help you to be like Christ in everything. Study the Word so that you can learn to be like Christ.

15

KNOWING CHRIST

The apostle Paul is a good example of a believer who dedicated his life to not only knowing Christ but following and emulating Him, as we learned yesterday. He understood that we cannot be Christ-minded without knowing Him fully.

In **Philippians 3:10-11** he says, *"I want to know Christ – yes, to know the power of his resurrection and participation in his sufferings, becoming like him in his death, and so, somehow, attaining to the resurrection from the dead."*

Paul is impacted by these characteristics of Jesus' life, which motivate him in his Christian walk. First is the power of His resurrection, and secondly the suffering He went through before His death. These aspects of Jesus' life led Paul to desire to emulate Jesus, so that, after death, he also will be resurrected one day. Paul sees eternity in Christ, the overcomer of death. He too wants to be so successful that death cannot hold him down.

Jesus was motivated by love. He committed His life to redeeming a lost world, through suffering and dying on the cross in order to become the ransom for our salvation. Understanding this commitment should help believers in their love and commitment to such a Saviour. Paul's prayer is to know Him more and understand His nature, which made Him so resilient under extreme pain that He chose to suffer death so that we do not suffer eternal death. The end result was a resurrection from the very thing that sought to exterminate Him.

If we fully understand the power of the resurrection, we will believe Jesus when He says we must not fear those who can only kill the body but never the soul. *"Do not be afraid of those who kill the body but cannot kill the soul. Rather, be afraid of the One who can destroy both soul and body in hell"* (**Matthew 10:28**). The life of a believer is in the soul. Our relationship with God is through our souls, not the flesh. God can destroy both the body and the soul. This helps us to honour and obey God rather than fear men.

This was the attitude of the early apostles and they were successful in their faith. Peter and the apostles said, *"We must obey God rather than human beings!"* (**Acts 5:29**). If we understand this, we can agree with Paul in his question in **Romans 8:35**: *"Who shall separate us from the love of Christ? Shall trouble or hardship or persecution or famine or nakedness or danger or sword?"*

In verse 37, Paul answers himself: *"No, in all these things we are more than conquerors through him who loved us."* This will also spur us to seek to know Jesus in our faith, with an understanding of the power of Jesus Christ. He helps us to obey God through His example.

Knowing Jesus and the power of His resurrection bolsters our confidence in His deliverance. Knowing the fellowship of His suffering helps us cope with suffering as well, and prepares us for eternity. Many believers backslide under immense pressure and persecution. In the end they lose out on the victory and glory of the resurrection. Knowing and emulating the path of Jesus will lead us to His glory and reward.

> ### REFLECTION TIME
>
> Make it your prayer to know Jesus more, through times of joy and through negative circumstances of your life. Ask God to show you what Jesus lost for us to know Him. Also ask God to show you what Jesus gained in the end as a result of His obedience. Following that way will make you successful in your faith walk. Remember His words in **John 14:6**: *"I am the way and the truth and the life. No one comes to the Father except through me."* Paul wanted to attain the resurrection like Jesus, and get to the Father. You too must get to the Father through knowing Jesus.

16

BEING HONEST IN ALL THINGS

Honesty is one characteristic that is lacking in many Christians today. This unfortunately affects the testimony of Jesus very negatively. Honesty must be a way of life for all in order for peace, love and trust to prevail. Alexander Pope, an 18th-century English poet once said, *"An honest man is the noblest work of God."* Believers are God's workmanship or handiwork, according to **Ephesians 2:10**. We should be honest in all things.

The apostle Paul reiterates this point in his letter to the Philippians in chapter 2, verse 15, urging them to *"become blameless and pure, 'children of God without fault in a warped and crooked generation.' Then you will shine among them like stars in the sky."* The law in the book of Leviticus sought to engrain honesty in the lives of people: *"Do not steal. Do not lie. Do not deceive one another"* (**Leviticus 19:11**).

Have you ever been tempted not to pay for something, to lie or to pick up something that does not belong to you? Have you ever been tempted not to be truthful at work, at home or worse still, at church? Have you ever been dishonest about your feelings? All these are integrity issues and many people struggle with them. God wants us to be honest in all things. **Proverbs 12:22** says: *"The Lord detests lying lips, but he delights in people who are trustworthy."* Look into your heart and ask God to help you to be honest in all things.

Being a follower of Jesus requires a lot of soul-searching and a continual review of our approach to life. The book of Romans says we must not conform to the pattern of this world (**Romans 12:2**), which is riddled with dishonesty. If we are to avoid becoming worldly we must learn to live by the Spirit, as Paul says, *"...live by the Spirit, and you will not gratify the desires of the flesh. For the flesh desires what is contrary to the Spirit, and the Spirit what is contrary to the flesh"* (**Galatians 5:17**).

The desire of the Spirit is for us to be honest. The life of honesty is a spiritual life. Jesus said that God is looking for those who will worship Him in spirit and in truth (**John 4:23**). This means we must be honest in all things. A Christian's usefulness to God is directly proportionate to his honesty. Never allow yourself to be trapped or deceived into anything that is unethical or dishonest and immoral, no matter how appealing it may seem. You will pay the cost if you do! Judas probably thought the 30 pieces of silver would transform him into a rich and contented man, but he was never able to spend a penny of that money. **Proverbs 13:11** warns about dishonest gains. Determine to be an honest Christian and trust God to elevate you, rather than giving in to what might seem to be a quicker but dishonest route.

Scripture also teaches us to avoid the company of dishonest people because they tend to influence us the wrong way. As you consider being honest, review some of your friendships if you want to be successful in this area. *"Bad company corrupts good character"* (**1 Corinthians 15:33**).

REFLECTION TIME

Look back into your life and repent where you have been dishonest in the past. Ask the Lord to forgive you and begin to review your associations. Cut off corrupt relationships and ask God to lead you into friendships that will help you to be honest.

17

CONDUCTIING YOUR LIFE WELL

The mistake many Christians make is to consider church as something that they go to rather than something they are. This results in confusion and double standards, where people want to showcase their faith in the church on a Sunday morning but live like the world on other days.

This confuses people and gives them a wrong understanding of the life of faith. Successful Christians have one lifestyle that cuts across their day-to-day lives, including the days they attend church. They conduct their lives well all the time.

Paul sums up the life of faith in these words: *"A bishop then must be blameless, the husband of one wife, temperate, sober-minded, of good behaviour, hospitable, able to teach; not given to wine, not violent, not greedy for money, but gentle, not quarrelsome, not covetous; one who rules his own house well, having his children in submission with all reverence (for if a man does not know how to rule his own house, how will he take care of the church of God?)..."* (**1 Timothy 3:2-5**, NKJV). This does not mean that other believers can live as they please. No! We all must behave like the bishops, because that is the standard of Jesus Christ.

Godly order must first be established in our own lives, through our character and conduct as families, before we can try to establish it in the church. As believers we are supposed to be preaching to others, *"Go into the world and preach the gospel..."* But we cannot preach what we do not practise. Preaching what we are not practising is hypocrisy.

The crowd that watched Jesus being crucified mockingly accused Him of hypocrisy in **Matthew 27:42**: *"He saved others... but he can't save himself!"* The way we run or rule our lives and homes must reflect the faith we profess, otherwise the world will question our sincerity. We are in the same position as the bishops Paul is talking about because we too preach to others – with both our lives and our words.

Our conduct and the conduct of our children should reflect a good testimony about our faith. If we behave contrary to what Paul says in **1 Timothy 3:2-5**, our children will not follow Christ's example in their lives. The reason why many children of Christians do not embrace the faith is because the parents have not demonstrated the life of a believer as required by this scripture. They compromise in their behaviour at home. This then complicates everything else they try to do in the name of faith. As a result, the church is losing its appeal and significance.

As we seek to walk closely with God, our homes and families cannot be left behind. It is important for us to realise that the way we rule our lives, our homes and our children will either help our cause in the church or hinder it.

REFLECTION TIME

How is your home ruled? Do your children understand the significance of your faith in your home? Are you conducting yourself with temperance? Are you sober-minded? Are you well behaved at home? How about wine, violence, greed and quarrelling? Children will copy you! Ask God to help you in these areas, so that your ministry is not diluted.

18

MANAGING YOUR THOUGHTS

A thought is an idea or opinion produced by thinking, or occurring suddenly in the mind. Our environment tends to contribute to our thought process, giving us positive or negative thoughts. Thoughts are crucial to a man's character and behaviour. If we want to be successful in our Christian walk, our thoughts must be checked regularly.

Proverbs 23:7 teaches, *"... as he thinks in his heart, so is he..."* (NKJV). This means that the character of a man, his behaviour and actions, are the sum total of his thoughts. This character influences the condition and circumstances of his life. Thoughts must not just be watched but must be moderated too.

Writing to the Philippians, the apostle Paul taught them how to think right: *"Finally, brothers and sisters, whatever is true, whatever is noble, whatever is right, whatever is pure, whatever is lovely, whatever is admirable – if anything is excellent or praiseworthy – think about such things"* (**Philippians 4:8**).

Here we are shown how to mould and fashion our thoughts in order to have a godly thought life. We must learn to think good things, pure things, right things, noble things and lovely things. Anything outside this must be removed from our thinking process if we want to remain godly.

This is how Christ thinks and He wants us to emulate Him. In **2 Corinthians 10:4-5** we are taught: *"The weapons we fight with are not the weapons of the world. On the contrary, they have divine power to demolish strongholds. We demolish arguments and every pretension that sets itself up against the knowledge of God, and we take captive every thought to make it obedient to Christ."*

Thoughts must be taught to obey Christ. They must be captured by the Word and shown the light of the Word, otherwise they will keep on arguing for the flesh. Our thoughts must line up with the Spirit of Christ if we want to be successful Christians. **1 Corinthians 2:16** says: *"But we have the mind of Christ."* How does the mind of Christ think? What does the mind of Christ think? What does the mind of Christ meditate on? All these questions can be answered by looking at the lifestyle of Jesus Christ... *"For as a man thinks in his heart, so is he."*

Learn to feed your thoughts with the Word of God. That way, you begin to think like God. Joshua was told to think about the Word day and night: *"Keep this Book of the Law always on your lips; meditate on it day and night, so that you may be careful to do everything written in it. Then you will be prosperous and successful"* (**Joshua 1:8**). Our behaviour and actions are a result of our thoughts! Good and godly thoughts will make you successful in your faith walk. David also says, *"May these words of my mouth and this meditation of my heart be pleasing in your sight, Lord, my Rock and my Redeemer"* (**Psalm 19:14**). This should be our daily prayer.

REFLECTION TIME

What do you meditate on day and night? That is what you will do. God wants us to do His will and that is found in the Word. Studying the Word will give you something good to think about. It will give you something pure to think about. It will give you something right to think about. Pray and ask God to help you capture every ungodly thought. Ask for help to bring your thoughts in obedience to Christ. Ask for help to apply the Word.

19

A Right Heart Attitude

Matthew 5 gives us the eight beatitudes of Jesus Christ. These teach us about the important attitudes those who believe in Jesus should display in their lifestyle. In verse 8, Jesus says: *"Blessed are the pure in heart, for they will see God."*

This is not the first time the Bible teaches about this important attitude in the life of a believer. King David valued the importance of heart purity as well: *"Who may ascend the mountain of the Lord? Who may stand in his holy place? The one who has clean hands and a pure heart..."* (**Psalm 24:3-4**).

Jesus promised that those who are pure in heart would see the Lord. David, on the other hand, suggested that those who will have fellowship with the Lord on His holy mountain are those with clean hands and a pure heart.

To be pure in heart means to be clean, blameless and unstained from guilt. Being pure in heart involves having a singleness of heart that is focused on God. A pure heart has no hypocrisy. It has no guile. A pure heart has no hidden motives. Such a heart is marked by transparency and a strong desire to please God at all times. Speaking on purity, the apostle Paul says: *"To the pure, all things are pure, but to those who are corrupted and do not believe, nothing is pure. In fact, both their minds and consciences are corrupted. They claim to know God, but by their actions they deny him. They are detestable, disobedient and unfit for doing anything good"* (**Titus 1:15-16**).

A pure heart will make us obedient to God. Our lives will reflect a fear and appreciation for God and His Word. The mind of the pure is undefiled; they are clean and godly. David always yearned and prayed for a pure heart. The heart purity song by Brian Doerksen can help us in our prayer as we ask for heart purity:

Purify my heart,
Let me be as gold and precious silver.
Purify my heart,
Let me be as gold, pure gold.
Refiner's fire,
My heart's one desire

Is to be holy, holy;
Set apart for You, Lord.

I choose to be holy, holy;
Set apart for You, my Master,
Ready to do Your will.

This is the prayer that will help you see God.

> **REFLECTION TIME**
>
> Take time to examine your heart. Allow the Holy Spirit to search your heart and respond to His promptings. Should there be anything you need to deal with, ask the Lord to help you empty all the contents of your heart. Ask Him to help you to be the overseer and manager of what goes in and out of your heart on a daily basis. Guard your heart diligently, and don't allow anyone else to determine the contents of your heart!

20

BEING DOERS OF THE WORD

One of the greatest challenges of a believer lies between the Word they know and the application of that Word. James calls it "doing" the Word in **James 1:22-24** (NKJV): *"But be doers of the word, and not hearers only, deceiving yourselves. For if anyone is a hearer of the word and not a doer, he is like a man observing his natural face in a mirror; for he observes himself, goes away, and immediately forgets what kind of man he was."*

The Bible also says we are a new creation, a brand new person! Doing the Word should keep us mindful of the transformation Christ has made in us, so we can continue to be conscious of it. Doing the Word helps us to maintain and remember the work of Christ in our lives. **Matthew 3:8** calls it producing fruit *"in keeping with repentance"*.

Forgetting what Jesus has done results in us going back to that life of sin, as **2 Peter 2:22** says. James further tells us that those who are doers of the Word are blessed in what they do (**James 1:25**). Here is a way to blessing – just do what the Word says.

Jesus talks about the same thing when teaching His disciples: *"If you love me, keep my commands"* (**John 14:15**). In other words, do what I tell you. In another scripture, **Matthew 15:8**, Jesus bemoans those who don't obey Him: *"These people honour me with their lips, but their hearts are far from me."* Here we understand that doing the Word honours Jesus. We don't honour Him in songs only. We honour Him by doing what He says.

How far is your heart from Jesus? You can measure this distance by how often you keep His Word or do what He tells you to do. When we keep the words of Jesus we honour God because God wants us to do what Jesus told us to do. On the mountain of transfiguration, God told the three disciples, *"This is my Son, whom I love. Listen to him!"* (**Mark 9:7**).

Being a doer keeps us close to the heart of God and aids our transformation process. When Jesus asked the rich young ruler to *"go, sell your possessions and give to the poor"*, the young man struggled to do what Jesus asked (**Matthew 19:21**). He found it too difficult and went away sorrowful. Sometimes what Jesus wants us to do is not easy, but He still wants us to trust Him and obey.

REFLECTION TIME

Ask God to help you to be a doer of the Word, as you work on walking with God. Look into areas where God has asked you to do something and you have not followed through. Rectify it and begin to honour God with your obedience.

21

APPLYING GOD'S WISDOM

Wisdom is one of the fundamental principles for living a successful Christian life. Joshua, the man who led the children of Israel after Moses, is described as wise in **Deuteronomy 34:9**: *"Now Joshua son of Nun was filled with the spirit of wisdom... So the Israelites listened to him..."* The children of Israel listened to the wisdom of Joshua and trusted him for guidance and leadership in a foreign land.

People in our families and communities will listen to us if we have wisdom. The Queen of Sheba travelled all the way from Ethiopia just to listen to the wisdom of Solomon (**1 Kings 10:4**). The Bible tells us that *"the Lord gives wisdom; from his mouth come knowledge and understanding"* (**Proverbs 2:6**). As Christians we have the wisdom of God at our disposal and we must begin to use it to lead our families and communities.

People need understanding and counsel in many areas of their lives. Let us begin to ask God to give us the spirit of wisdom. Joseph was wise, that is why he was elevated to second in charge in a foreign land. Daniel was wise, and rose to prominence in Babylon. Nehemiah was wise because God gave him wisdom, and he was able to rebuild Jerusalem. **James 1:5** says: *"If any of you lacks wisdom, you should ask God, who gives generously to all without finding fault, and it will be given to you."* Proverbs also tells us that the Lord gives wisdom. We should ask for wisdom and God will give it to us generously.

Many of the problems we encounter in life are due to our lack of wisdom. The world respects wisdom because it is the effective use of knowledge. Wisdom is also the key to building healthy relationships. The wisdom of God will help us take away confusion and replace it with soundness in our homes and communities.

But God does not just dish His wisdom out in the marketplace. We must desire wisdom and ask for it, and do all it takes for us to apply it in our day-to-day lives. There are candidates for wisdom and you are one of them, because Jesus lives in you. Ask God for wisdom and use it to transform your community. Let people travel to come and receive the wisdom of God from you. God will be glorified when you walk wisely.

REFLECTION TIME

Look around for wise people and begin to associate with them. Study the Word and seek out wise people in the Bible in order to learn from them. We are told that the wise men from the east visited Jesus in Matthew 2. When you are wise, you will be acknowledged wherever you visit. Ask the Lord to impart His wisdom to you so that you may be a blessing to your community. Learn to deal wisely with all at all times.

22
Developing The Fruit Of The Spirit

Walking in the spirit is a concept that Paul taught the Galatian church. He gave this teaching because it is only by walking in the spirit that we do not yield to the flesh. Most of our relationships are hurt and affected because we relate carnally, and we respond to issues in a carnal way.

Paul then says we must have the fruit of the Spirit in us so that we may not be conceited and become slaves of the flesh. To be conceited is to be excessively proud and selfish. This type of character does not align with the Christian lifestyle based on biblical principles. To avoid this, we must develop the fruit of the Spirit. The fruit of the Spirit basically refers to behaviour that is regulated and submitted to the Word of God.

Paul also says that when we develop the fruit of the Spirit we will not provoke one another. To provoke is to stimulate or give rise to a reaction or emotion, typically a strong or an unwelcome one. Have you ever provoked anyone before? Such provocations among Christians lead to fights and arguments in the body of Christ. To avoid this, Paul says we must develop the fruit of the Spirit.

A fruit does not eat itself; it's for the benefit of others. A tree does not show off its fruit and does not call everyone to come and admire it. A tree does not sit under its own shade for protection from the heat. Both the fruit and the tree are for the benefit of others. When we develop the fruit of the Spirit, those in relationship with us will benefit and God is glorified in the process.

As we pray, let us consider all these things so that we may be successful in our spiritual walk. *"But the fruit of the Spirit is love, joy, peace, forbearance, kindness, goodness, faithfulness, gentleness and self-control"* (**Galatians 5:22-23**). In verses 25-26, Paul suggests: *"Since we live by the Spirit, let us keep in step with the Spirit. Let us not become conceited, provoking and envying each other."* We must walk in the Spirit because that is the only way to avoid fulfilling the lusts of the flesh.

REFLECTION TIME

Look into your life and begin to identify areas where you have walked in the flesh, envied, provoked others, or even became conceited, and ask for forgiveness. Pray about the fruit of the Spirit and measure your growth in all of them. Ask God to help you to develop them continuously.

23

THE FRUIT OF GOODNESS

The fruit of the Spirit must be continually cultivated. No farmer cultivates a tree once and expects it to carry on producing fruit for ever. There are elements that affect trees, like weather, diseases, storms and so on. So developing the fruit of the Spirit requires a lot of effort and determination. The fruit of goodness is important and is being challenged today

The Prophet Isaiah points this out in **Isaiah 5:20**: *"Woe to those who call evil good and good evil, who put darkness for light and light for darkness, who put bitter for sweet and sweet for bitter."* We can see from this that good can easily be manipulated and, if we are not discerning, we ourselves can begin to call evil good and good evil. Goodness comes from God, because God is good. According to the world, goodness can be relative – depending on different people's opinions of what is good. But the goodness of the Spirit comes from this fundamental attribute of God, who has no evil in Him.

In **2 Timothy 3:1-9**, Paul says that, in the last days, those who are evil will despise the fruit of goodness: *"People will be lovers of themselves, lovers of money, boastful, proud, abusive, disobedient to their parents, ungrateful, unholy, without love, unforgiving, slanderous, without self-control, brutal, not lovers of the good..."* All these traits are the opposite of good, and some of us as Christians have been guilty of them.

Jesus was different! In **Acts 10:38**, we are told that He *"went around doing good"*. For us to challenge the apostasy of the last days, we need to develop the fruit of goodness that was characteristic of Jesus Christ. Such goodness is the opposite of the sinfulness that Paul mentions in **2 Timothy 3**. It has to do with the state or quality of being good. It's about generosity and kindness, it's about moral excellence, piety and virtue. Jesus was approved as good during His time on earth. This goodness must be consciously and steadily maintained. We should not be good one day and different the next. David says, *"Surely your goodness and love will follow me all the days of my life"* (**Psalm 23:6**). True goodness is displayed in spite of evil influences around us.

Romans 12:9 states that *"love must be sincere"* and implores us to *"hate what is evil; cling to what is good"*. **Galatians 6:10** challenges us to exercise the fruit of goodness: *"Therefore, as we have opportunity, let us do good to all people, especially to those who belong to the family of believers."* We must learn to test things and only hold onto what is good, according to **1 Thessalonians 5:21**. We cannot hold on to goodness if we do not develop this attitude in our day-to-day living. It's very easy to be proud and selfish. It's very easy to boast and be unforgiving, but that is not goodness.

We must learn goodness from God, because *"no one is good – except God alone"* (**Mark 10:18**). We will learn this trait from the Word of God. We can ask the Holy Spirit to help us develop the fruit of goodness.

> **REFLECTION TIME**
>
> What kind of person are you? Are you good in your conduct, speech, in your attitudes, and in relating to those you don't like? As believers we are expected to do good all the time. Ask God to help you apply His Word and teaching in your conduct.

24

THE FRUIT OF GENTLENESS

In many places in the world, men are usually referred to as 'gentlemen'. This is not the fruit of the Spirit the apostle Paul is talking about, *"But the fruit of the Spirit is love, joy, peace, forbearance, kindness, goodness, faithfulness, gentleness and self-control"* (**Galatians 5:22-23**).

The word gentleness in Greek is 'prautes', which emphasises the divine origin of the meekness in someone. This word refers to 'gentle strength'; it expresses power with reserve and gentleness. Jesus was gentle in the way He handled the Roman soldiers and Jews who mocked Him and spat on His face. This is how Isaiah describes His gentleness: *"He was oppressed and afflicted, yet he did not open his mouth; he was led like a lamb to the slaughter, and as a sheep before its shearers is silent, so he did not open his mouth."*

Jesus had the capacity to destroy all those who crucified Him but He was gentle; He was able to express His power with reserve and gentleness.

For us as believers, gentleness should be understood from Jesus' example and His teachings on how to live with others. For example, Jesus said: *"But I tell you, do not resist an evil person. If anyone slaps you on the right cheek, turn to them the other cheek also. And if anyone wants to sue you and take your shirt, hand over your coat as well. If anyone forces you to go one mile, go with them two miles"* (**Matthew 5:39-41**). This might not literally happen to you, but the lesson is to approach adversity with a humble and gentle heart instead of being reactionary and aggressive.

Jesus was successful by utilising the fruit of gentleness in situations where He could have easily lashed out and killed somebody. The apostle Paul also teaches this important principle to the young minister, Timothy. He says: *"As a prisoner for the Lord, then, I urge you to live a life worthy of the calling you have received. Be completely humble and gentle; be patient, bearing with one another in love. Make every effort to keep the unity of the Spirit through the bond of peace"* (**Ephesians 4:1-3**).

Gentleness is essential for us to keep unity and peace. Gentleness is necessary if we are to exercise patience. All believers must develop the fruit of gentleness if the church is to remain united.

REFLECTION TIME

Pray that the Lord will help you to develop gentleness in your dealings with people. How easy is it to turn another cheek? How about giving your jacket when your shirt has already been taken away, or walking an extra mile after being forced to walk another? These are instances that require gentleness from you. It's not about what you do externally, but about the attitude in which you do it.

25

THE FRUIT OF FAITHFULNESS

You may be asking yourself, "How can faithfulness be considered a fruit of the Spirit?" Oh yes, it is! Faithfulness is the foundation of every relationship. It is a characteristic of God's ethical nature and it shows us His consistency in commitment to His promises. Faithfulness is an aspect of God's truth and character and we need this in our relationships for us to be successful.

No one wants to keep company with a liar. No one wants to work with someone who will change his mind when we are entirely depending on him sticking to our agreement. One of the reasons for divorce and church splits is a lack of faithfulness. God is faithful! *"O Lord God of Heaven's Armies! Where is there anyone as mighty as you, O Lord? You are entirely faithful"* (**Psalm 89:8, NLT**).

Faithfulness is at the heart of all that God is and does. We are expected to be the same. His truthfulness, His holiness, His love and righteousness and all His other attributes ensure His faithfulness. That is why the Bible wants us to develop these attributes through prayer, study, repentance, meditation and all disciplines. We must be like God. In His faithfulness God does not fail us, according to **1 Peter 4:19**. We must also not fail others. We fail them because we do not understand the importance of faithfulness in our lives.

Determine to develop faithfulness as a child of a faithful God. **1 Thessalonians 5:23-24** says, *"Now may the God of peace make you holy in every way, and may your whole spirit and soul and body be kept blameless until our Lord Jesus Christ comes again. God will make this happen, for he who calls you is faithful."* God is faithful and He wants us to be like Him. Jesus said, *"Anyone who has seen me has seen the Father"* (**John 14:9**), and Jesus was faithful like His Father. We must also be faithful like Jesus in the same manner that the Father is faithful. Faithfulness is a fruit of the Spirit and **John 14** tells us that God is a Spirit. Faithfulness as a fruit of the Spirit comes from the character of God, because the Holy Spirit is God.

Faithfulness is evidence that God is in you. A simple biblical definition of faithfulness is having or showing true and constant support or loyalty, deserving trust and keeping your promises.

How far are you from this definition in your dealings with family, friends, church, work and your community? God can help you change, because developing this fruit is very important.

> **REFLECTION TIME**
>
> Ask God for forgiveness for being unfaithful (we all have been in some way or other) and for His help to begin to value this attribute. Develop ways to check yourself daily on keeping your word and loyalty. You will be more successful if people can trust you. Pray for change and work on it in these coming months. *"God is not human, that he should lie, not a human being, that he should change his mind. Does he speak and then not act? Does he promise and not fulfil?"* (**Numbers 23:19**). Measure yourself against this word and begin a journey towards faithfulness.

26

THE FRUIT OF PATIENCE

One of the fruits of the Spirit in **Galatians 5** is *'patience'* or *'forbearance'*. Some Bible translations say *'long-suffering'*.

Patience is a very important attribute to be developed by all. Patience can be defined as the capacity to accept or tolerate delay, problems or suffering without becoming annoyed or anxious. On the other hand, the dictionary defines the word 'long-suffering' as showing patience in spite of trouble, or challenges, especially those caused by other people. This shows that long-suffering and patience work hand in hand.

Have you ever been in a situation where you feel something is delaying you or getting in your way? Did you want to take things into your own hands? Have you been in a situation where you thought people were not shaping up the way you would like them to? The Bible admonishes us to be patient if we want to be successful in our relationships in life.

A typical example of this is found in Jesus' parable in **Luke 13:6-9**: *"A man had a fig-tree growing in his vineyard, and he went to look for fruit on it but did not find any. So he said to the man who took care of the vineyard, 'For three years now I've been coming to look for fruit on this fig-tree and haven't found any. Cut it down! Why should it use up the soil?'"*

Verse 8 then tells us that the man who cared for the vineyard asked the owner to exercise patience. How many times have you cut the tree down because you thought it was taking up space? How many friends have you lost because you thought it was too much effort to keep them? How many homes are broken today because someone lost patience with their spouse or partner. Patience teaches us to be tolerant and wait a little longer. Patience is about suffering long, to allow God to work for you.

Sometimes you develop patience by talking to someone who can encourage you, as in verse 8: *"'Sir... leave it alone for one more year, and I'll dig round it and fertilise it. If it bears fruit next year, fine! If not, then cut it down.'"* Some situations just need us to fertilise them, instead of giving up due to impatience.

Being tolerant to challenges and to endure them for longer develops patience. With prayer and God's help, things can change. We must not be too quick to cut down the tree. You may just destroy a tree that could have been the foundation for your success. Paul says love is patient. We must learn to be patient with people.

Moses had to endure hardship from Pharaoh until God finished what He wanted to do. David was patient with King Saul. **James 1:4** teaches us to *"let patience have its perfect work, that you may be perfect and complete, lacking nothing"* (NKJV). The Message version says: *"You know that under pressure, your faith-life is forced into the open and shows its true colours. So don't try to get out of anything prematurely. Let it do its work so you become mature and well-developed, not deficient in any way."* The fruit of patience will make you well-developed, mature, and successful.

> ### REFLECTION TIME
> If you were to count the cost of your impatience, what valuable things have you lost? Pray and ask God to help you develop patience with people and circumstances. Sometimes certain delays are merely protecting you from a disastrous future. Ask God to help you to develop patience and long-suffering in your daily life.

27

Practising Kindness

"*But the fruit of the Spirit is... kindness...*" (**Galatians 5:22**). Do you consider yourself to be kind? Have others benefited from your kindness? Kindness is an expression of God's love and helps people to cope and make it through, with the help of others. David says of God, "*Your lovingkindness is better than life...*" (**Psalm 63:3**).

When you are kind, you become a lifeline to others. When you are kind, people will want to be around you. David so longed for God's kindness that he wrote, "*Early will I seek You; my soul thirsts for You; my flesh longs for You... So I have looked for You in the sanctuary...*" (**Psalm 63:1-2, NKJV**).

Kind people are like a well of fresh water in the hot desert. Kindness gives meaning and purpose to our lives. It helps us out of our troubles and makes us feel good about ourselves. God wants us to make others feel good about themselves and to help them out of their troubles. If we are kind in that way, then when we are in trouble, they will help us in return because of the kindness they received from us. Kindness is a help chain that must continue to run and flourish. If everyone refused to be kind, soon the whole world would be in trouble!

Kindness requires sensitivity and love. It requires an understanding that we are all humans and can experience problems. Kindness is that quality of being friendly and generous when the situation requires. It is that heart of being considerate and caring which can mean the world for someone who needs it.

Kindness is a fruit God uses for us to meet the needs of others. It is an opportunity to show our humanity and sensitivity. The Bible encourages us to be kind to one another and to strangers. My daughter told me that life is so unpredictable sometimes, which is why we must learn to be kind. One day someone you helped before will help you. That is why the Bible says, "*Do not withhold good from those to whom it is due, when it is in your power to act*" (**Proverbs 3:27**). What is in your power today may be in someone else's power tomorrow. That is why it is very important for you to be kind. We are told that love is kind (**1 Corinthians 13:4**). If you have love you will show kindness. We must love everybody so we must be kind to everybody. This helps us to be successful in the way we influence people for Christ because they will always respect us. Kind people are the best kind of people. No wonder God wants us to be kind. He wants us to be the best.

REFLECTION TIME

Ask God to give you a kind heart. Ask Him to make you sensitive and considerate. Read through the life of Jesus to learn how kind He was and begin to desire it daily. God will answer you and soon you will hear testimonies of your kindness from places you never imagined.

28

PRACTISING SELF-CONTROL

Self-control is basically about controlling certain emotions and behaviours so that they don't drag you into sin. Exercising self-control is in the nature of God, who made us in His likeness. This is why we must also learn self-control.

There are many areas where we need to control ourselves. One such area is our words. How many times have you regretted uttering certain statements? You failed to control your mouth and ended up destroying a valuable relationship or hurting someone. Many unnecessary wars have started because of careless words. **Proverbs 18:21** says, *"The tongue has the power of life and death, and those who love it will eat its fruit."* You have a responsibility to control the words you speak. In **Matthew 12:36-37**, the Bible warns us that we will have to account for every idle word we speak. This should make us realise that some words will cause us to sin against one another, so learning to check what we say before we say it is the only way to overcome careless words. Self-control is a fruit of the Spirit that is helpful to you as an individual, but also minimises the pain of others.

How about sexual desires? Failing to control them is dangerous. The worst result of uncontrolled sexual desire is rape, but there are many other consequences. Rape may result in a prison sentence, but other sexual sins can force you to spend your entire life in a prison of your own making. Pornography, for example, is very addictive and can dominate your life. Sexual diseases are also the consequence of a lack of self-control of sexual desires.

The greatest of all consequences, though, is mentioned in **Revelation 21:8:** *"But the cowardly, the unbelieving, the vile, the murderers, the sexually immoral... they will be consigned to the fiery lake of burning sulphur."* This is hell forever, due to a failure in self-control, so controlling ourselves in this area is not an option!

Self-control is also required in our emotions. Murder is a result of the emotion of anger, which is why we are taught, *"'In your anger do not sin': do not let the sun go down while you are still angry"* **(Ephesians 4:26)**. So it is possible to be angry and not sin, but this can only happen if you are able to control yourself. Self-control is something we have to learn and practise continually, as well as prayerfully.

Other areas where we need self-control is in our use of money. Lack of control leads to debt and struggles in families, which in turn causes family breakdowns and unnecessary bondages when borrowing from others. A lack of control of the desire for the things we want – greed and envy – also contributes to money problems, even causing someone to fall into theft or gambling. Self-control is a fruit of the Spirit we must develop in order to avoid debt and poverty.

There are many areas in our lives where we need to apply this important principle. Consider your thoughts. How much goes through your mind daily? If you lose control of that you can end up in trouble, even losing your very mind. **Philippians 4:8** teaches us to control our thoughts by concentrating on positive things: *"Whatever is true, whatever is noble, whatever is right, whatever is pure, whatever is lovely, whatever is admirable – if anything is excellent or praiseworthy – think about such things."*

Friends and acquaintances must also be checked, otherwise they can lead you into trouble. Bad company always corrupts good morals. Many people have got into trouble because of wrong influences from friends. They failed to say no to certain ideas from friends, then ended up in regret when things went wrong.

Have you ever thought that sleep should be controlled? Oh yes! Some people fail to control their sleep, to the point where all they do is sleep all day. This leads to laziness, depression, unemployment and poverty. *"A little sleep, a little slumber, a little folding of hands to rest – and poverty will come on you like a thief..."* (**Proverbs 6:10-11**).

Time must also be controlled, otherwise you can lose time or just waste it on useless things. Have you noticed how much time you lose just watching TV? David says, *"Teach us to number our days, that we may gain a heart of wisdom"* (**Psalm 90:12**). Numbering our days means realising that time is precious and life is short, so we need to plan what we do rather than letting time just slip by. Perhaps you need to reassess the habits, pleasures and activities that take up time in your life? Or maybe you are spending too much time at work and not enough with the family? All these challenges require us to learn self-control. *"But the fruit of the Spirit is... self-control"* (**Galatians 5:22-23**).

Reflection Time

In which areas of your life have you lost control? You need to get it back before you get into trouble. Ask God for help as you pray, and also guard your heart and mind throughout the day as you seek to remain in control.

29

WALKING IN PEACE

The most common and familiar definition of peace is probably non-aggression and non-violence. That is the nature of the Christian faith: it is peaceful, not violent or aggressive. But Jesus did not promise us an absence of war, He promised us a kind of peace that the world cannot give (**John 14:27**) – an inner peace.

This kind of peace is a sense of calmness or restfulness, a supernatural inner stability given by God, even in the midst of storms.

When Jesus appeared to His disciples soon after the resurrection, His greeting was, *"Peace be with you!"* (**Luke 24:36**). The following verse explains why Jesus was offering them peace. The disciples were terrified because they thought Jesus was a ghost, so Jesus was calming them down. This was not the first time that Jesus had calmed the disciples' fear with the fruit of peace. In **Matthew 14:27** Jesus spoke to the fearful disciples, saying, *"Take courage! It is I. Don't be afraid."*

When you are disturbed you might panic, and then you are not in charge of your emotions; instead, your emotions take charge of you. The fruit of peace insulates our hearts, helping us to remain calm and hopeful. We should also be able to pass this restfulness and calmness to others. In **Matthew 10**, Jesus sends His disciples out to preach and tells them, *"If the home is deserving, let your peace rest on it..."* (verse 13). In other words, we must be able to bring peace wherever we go. But we cannot give what we do not have, so we must develop this fruit of the Spirit in our own lives. It helps us to be effective in places where we minister.

Peace will uphold you when your faith is shaken or when your life is threatened. In **John 14:27** Jesus says, *"Peace I leave with you; my peace I give you. I do not give to you as the world gives. Do not let your hearts be troubled and do not be afraid."* The fruit of peace helps in situations where fear wants to destabilise us. Jesus kept giving peace to the disciples when He saw that their faith was wavering. Isaiah says that Jesus is not only the *"Wonderful Counsellor, Mighty God, Everlasting Father"* but the *"Prince of Peace"* (**Isaiah 9:6**).

The fruit of peace is the person of Jesus Himself, living in us by the Holy Spirit. He gives us confidence in who we are and the authority God has given us. **Colossians 3:15** says, *"Let the peace of Christ rule in your hearts, since as members of one body you were called to peace."* Walking in peace is part of our calling. This fruit removes strife and contentions, bringing unity and oneness in the body.

Ephesians 2:14 says Jesus Himself is our peace, and in **Philippians 4:7** Paul says the peace of God will guard our hearts and minds. How peaceful are you? How often do you pursue peace with others? Are you at peace with yourself? Do you have peace with God?

> ### Reflection Time
> Ask God to help you to develop a peaceful heart. Ask for stability and faith so that you are not easily shaken. Pray to be a peacemaker. **Matthew 5:9** says, *"Blessed are the peacemakers, for they will be called children of God."*

30

WALKING IN LOVE

"*But the fruit of the Spirit is love...*" (**Galatians 5:22**). In **1 Corinthians 13**, Paul teaches about the true essence of love: *"If I speak in the tongues of men or of angels, but do not have love, I am only a resounding gong or a clanging cymbal. If I have the gift of prophecy and can fathom all mysteries and all knowledge, and if I have a faith that can move mountains, but do not have love, I am nothing. If I give all I possess to the poor and give over my body to hardship that I may boast, but do not have love, I gain nothing"* (verses 1-3). From these verses we see that activities and achievements without love are worth nothing. Love is key to all we do, so developing it must be a daily priority. In verses 4-8, Paul moves on to show us a few characteristics of love that must be developed. First of all, he says love is patient. If you lack patience towards others, it means you are not walking in love. Developing patience is developing an aspect of love, and this will be profitable to you and to others.

The next attribute of love that Paul lists is kindness. This is self-explanatory – everyone understands that to be kind is to be loving. Thirdly, he says, love is not envious. Envy is a feeling or an act of jealous resentment towards someone or towards their achievements. Have you been envious of someone before? Then you were not walking in the spirit, you were not walking in love.

Then Paul mentions that love does not boast and is not proud. Boasting is a result of pride and arrogance. The Bible tells us that God resists the proud (**James 4:6**). The remaining qualities of love that Paul gives are: *"It does not dishonour others, it is not self-seeking, it is not easily angered, it keeps no record of wrongs. Love does not delight in evil but rejoices with the truth. It always protects, always trusts, always hopes, always perseveres. Love never fails..."* (verses 5-8).

When the Bible tells us to *"live by the spirit"* in **Galatians 5:16**, it means we must walk in love. Walking in love is exhibiting in our lives all these qualities that the apostle Paul talks about.

In verse 8 Paul tells us that love never fails – it is eternal! That's because God is love, and God is eternal. Jesus says He came to give us eternal life (**John 10:10**), but that life starts now – as we experience His love and share it with others.

Walking in love is a kingdom principle we all must strive to put into practice.

There is a lot that the Bible teaches us about love. In **Romans 12:9** we are told that our love must be without hypocrisy. That chapter goes on to give us other aspects of love that we must aim to develop as we learn to walk in love.

How is your love walk towards your Christian brothers and sisters and those around you? The standard has already been laid down in the Word. *"But the fruit of the Spirit is love..."*

REFLECTION TIME

Examine your love walk. Make an assessment, using the teaching from **1 Corinthians 13**, and begin to align your life according to those verses. Pray for God's help in all these aspects of love and determine to work on each and every one of them. It will lead you to God because God is love. Be watchful and be diligent to walk in love, so that you don't end up as a noisy cymbal and that all your efforts do not end up amounting to nothing.

OTHER BOOKS BY

The Fragrance of a Godly Woman
by Fatima Sibanda
ISBN: 978-0-9561175-0-2

Daughter Arise! Defy Your Limitations and Scale the Utmost Height
by Fatima Sibanda
ISBN: 978-0-9561175-4-0

The Value of Kindness
by Osien Sibanda
ISBN: 978-0-9561175-6-4

The Principles and Practice of Giving
by Osien Sibanda
ISBN: 978-0-9561175-1-9

The God Told Me Syndrome
by Osien Sibanda
ISBN: 978-0-9561175-2-6

Count the Cost
by Osien Sibanda
ISBN: 978-0-9561175-3-3

Your Path is Becoming Brighter
by Fatima Sibanda
ISBN: 978-0-9561175-7-1

For more information please contact info@sibandapublishing.com

www.ingramcontent.com/pod-product-compliance
Lightning Source LLC
Chambersburg PA
CBHW050606300426
44112CB00013B/2105